# ARRANGING
# FAUX FLOWERS & FOLIAGE

# ARRANGING
# FAUX FLOWERS
## & FOLIAGE

### 35 creative step-by-step projects

Linda Peterson

CICO BOOKS
LONDON  NEW YORK

This edition published in 2017 by CICO Books
An imprint of Ryland Peters & Small Ltd
20–21 Jockey's Fields      341 E 116th St
London WC1R 4BW      New York, NY 10029

www.rylandpeters.com

10 9 8 7 6 5 4 3 2 1

First published in 2008 by CICO Books as *Arranging Silk Flowers*

A CIP catalog record for this book is available from the Library of Congress and the British Library.

ISBN: 978 1 78249 481 2

Printed in China

Editor: Marie Clayton
Designer: Roger Hammond
Style photography: Emma Mitchell and Debbie Patterson
Step-by-step photography: Geoff Dann
Stylists: Rose Hammick and Emma Hardy

In-house editor: Anna Galkina
Art director: Sally Powell
Production controller: David Hearn
Publishing manager: Penny Craig
Publisher: Cindy Richards

# Contents

# Introduction

As I look back through photographs of when I was a child, I am reminded of my fascination with flowers. I was about six years old when I planted my first garden; I carefully loosened the soil and gently sprinkled a variety of flower seeds. After several days, there they were, tiny little seedlings popping forth from the soil. My flowers were born! I was fascinated—and what a joy it was when they rewarded me with a rainbow of colorful blossoms that I enjoyed over the hot summer months.

As I grew older, my Dad gave my garden a more prominent spot. This particular garden was a large round circle and my parents and I carefully planned the height of the flowers so that the taller ones were in the middle with the more delicate ones outlining the edges, giving the bed a beautiful border. Little did I know that way back then, I was already "arranging" flowers in my garden, giving attention to placement, color, and texture. When the flowers grew tall enough, I would hand-pick them, arrange them in my mother's glass vases, and display them in the house. Sadly, the beautiful bouquets didn't last that long after they were picked—they soon withered and died, and because of this faux flowers became an interest for me.

Faux flowers and plants, or "permanent botanicals," have made such a huge leap since way back then. A real effort has been put into creating florals that fool the senses both in appearance and in touch. There are many advantages to using faux flowers—consider a few of these for example: faux flowers and plants offer long-term savings over real flowers and plants because they require very little attention; you can go away on vacation without returning home to dead plants; faux flowers provide the look of real flowers, but allergy sufferers do not have to contend with the pollen; because there is no need to water faux flowers, you will never have water damage from overfilling your pots; faux flowers do not attract insects. And the best reason to create with faux flowers? You can change the arrangements around at any given time to meet your tastes and various décor styles!

You don't need a degree in floral arranging to create any of these arrangements. Even if you are just beginning, you will be amazed at how easy and gratifying the process is. In this book I share the techniques I've learned, some of which are quick and simple, others just a tad more complex, so that you can create beautiful faux arrangements to enrich your soul and give a touch of warmth to your home. As you handle the flowers, take a moment to admire their beauty, uniqueness, and inner meaning. You will find it a great stress reliever for your mind, body, and spirit.

Selection of faux florals can be daunting if you don't know what to look for, and there are a grades to choose from. Just remember, if it doesn't look real to you, it won't look real in the arrangement! Realistic faux flowers tend to be a bit higher in price, but in the long run they are cheaper than their fresh counterparts and will last a lifetime with proper care. Look for flowers that mimic the real ones closely, replicating textures and details such as veins. Stamens will be made in natural fibers rather than plastics, and stems should mimic real flowers in size and structure. Many stems have extra heavy wire inside to provide good support. Petals should not be ragged and torn, and they are often individually wired so that they can be arranged more naturally. Wired leaves are also important to achieve just the shape you need. As the saying goes, "You get what you pay for." Enjoy faux nature's wonders.

# The Basics

Floral arrangements can brighten any area of your home.
When choosing a design for a particular place, think about how it
will fit into the space available. Will it be seen from above—
if it is sitting on a low table, for instance? Or will it be a table
centerpiece and therefore on view all the way around?
In a high traffic area you'll want to make sure that none of the
floral stems stick out, which might cause the arrangement
to get knocked and fall. Do you want your arrangement to be an
accent or a focal point in the room? These are all factors
to consider, and there are also tips featured in the
Designs Elements section that will help you create an
arrangement that is just perfect for any area
of your home.

As with any project, there are a few staple materials and
techniques that you will need to be successful when you are
arranging florals. Many of these materials you may have
already laying around the house. In this chapter, I've covered
some of the basics to help you get started. Not all the
materials featured are used in the projects in this book, but you
should be aware that they are available in case you
come to need them in the future.

# The Language of Flowers

When I began creating the arrangements in this book, I couldn't help but think back to when I was a child, working in my garden. The idea of arranging flowers brought back many happy memories. I think of how flowers enriched my life then, how they decorate and bring warmth and feeling to my home now, how they make it a comfortable place to live. We are deeply blessed to be living in a world full of beauty and color!

Perhaps there are flowers that hold a special meaning or memory for you. Today we often send flowers to say, "I love you," or "I'm thinking of you." Flowers are uplifting to a dear friend or loved one in distress. We congratulate and celebrate with flowers. It's as if flowers have their own way of communicating our emotions.

The language of flowers is not something new: the idea of conveying messages with flowers was first brought to England in 1716 by Lady Mary Whortley Montagu, the wife of an English ambassador to Turkey. However, it was during the reign of Queen Victoria that the trend grew in popularity. Queen Victoria loved flowers and communicating through flowers became an obsession with the English. They grew them, wore them, used them in cosmetics, for cooking, and home decorating—they wore flowers more than they wore jewelry. Women and men, young and old, studied floral languages in order to become more fluent in meaning. It was during this time that simple messages were assigned to individual flowers.

This was a time in history when expressions of feeling were restricted by etiquette. Men and women, unable to express their feelings openly, used the beauty and color of flowers to send unspoken messages to one another—flowers became their avenue to express wishes, thoughts, and ideas discreetly. Careful attention and planning was given to the flower selection in a bouquet, in order to convey the appropriate sentiment, thought or wish. Presentation of the flowers was also important—gift givers could add even more meaning to their message, simply by the way in which the flowers were presented. For instance, if one were to receive an upside-down bouquet of flowers it would convey the opposite meaning; so a red rose would mean love, but upside down it would convey rejection. Oh! definitely not a pleasant thought at all! But instead of the negative, let's focus on the more positive aspects of flower giving and take a look at some of the good meanings of flowers. Remember, though, that over time some of the meanings have changed and the meaning

AGAPHANTHUS

COSMOS

CHRYSANTHEMUM

DAISY

may be different in different cultures. Here are a few of my favorites:

**Agapanthus** is a flower that I love, with its blue and purple, bell-like flowers. This flower derives its name from "agape" meaning love, and "anthos" meaning flower. Thus it is known as the flower of love. Agapeo means "to be contented with," which also gives the possible meaning "with this I am well pleased."

**Cosmos** gives a message of peacefulness. The delicate, gentle texture of its leaves is a favorite of mine to use when designing.

**Chrysanthemums** convey the meaning of being a wonderful friend. They can also symbolize cheerfulness.

**Daisies** were originally named from the Anglo-Saxon word "daes eage" or "day's eye," which refers to the way the flower opens and closes with the sun. This flower is known as a symbol of childhood innocence and can also be associated with simplicity and modesty. Heartbroken young women during the Victorian era, who wished to be loved again, would carry the daisy. A young maiden would pluck the daisy's petals one by one and sing, "He loves me, he loves me not," as each petal fell.

The last petal plucked predicted the future of their love.

**Daffodil** symbolizes regard: "You're the only one," or the "sun is always shining when I'm with you."

**Delphinium** means boldness. It is easy to see how this tall, fortress-like flower gives off the meaning of strength and boldness. I use it to add height and boldness to my designs as well.

**Forsythia** sends a message of anticipation. This must be true because, when I was a little girl, we had a forsythia bush in the corner of our yard. It was bright yellow, my favorite color; I loved the delicate yellow blooms and I waited with anticipation for its colorful display of beauty each spring.

**Geraniums** have long been a favorite of my mother. Geraniums have become part of the "welcome" that you receive when you arrive at her home and they symbolize comfort. When I think of the word "comfort," I think of the phrase "there's no place like home." There really is no place like the comfortable feeling of home and I also think of bringing comfort to a friend in distress, or one who has fallen ill.

**Hyacinth** is one of my favorite flowers and an indication that spring is on its way. It is a symbol for loveliness.

DELPHINIUM

FORSYTHIA

GERANIUM

HYACINTH

**Hydrangea**, unfortunately—while it is one of my favorite "mass" flowers—has the rather grim meaning of boastfulness.

**Iris** symbolizes a deep friendship, faith, and hope. These flowers would line my grandmother's yard each year, and as they bloom in my yard now I remember the time I spent with my Grandma, a "friendship that meant so much to me!"

**Ivy** became a romantic gesture and a feature in many wedding flowers, a tradition started by Queen Victoria. After the special day, the ivy was planted as a living reminder of the event. It is also associated with friendship.

**Lilacs** reflect youthful innocence.

**Lilies** can be seen in many varieties. The calla lily symbolizes beauty, while the tiger lily is a symbol of wealth and pride.

**Magnolias** are a symbol of perseverance.

**Orchids** derive their name from the Greek word "orchis," and there are almost 25,000 different types. A peculiar fact about the orchid is that for its seed to germinate it needs to be penetrated by fungus threads. Its history is rather unpleasant, because the flower was associated with lust, greed, and wealth. In more recent times, the orchid delivers a universal message of love, purity, wisdom, and thoughtfulness. The different colors can deliver strong messages: a pink orchid can signify affection, while the more popular orchids represent mature charm.

**Peonies** bloom each year in my garden. The blooms are delicate yet, but together they are powerful and a symbol of a happy marriage.

**Roses** are said to have appeared in Asian gardens more than 5,000 years ago—they were used primarily as ornamental decoration. It is said that Cleopatra scattered rose petals before Mark Antony's feet, and that Nero released

IVY

HYDRANGEA

IRIS

LILAC

LILY

ORCHID

roses from the ceiling during extravagant feasts. The rose is our most sentimental flower and symbol of love. A single rose can symbolize perpetual love, while two roses of any color joined together can convey a commitment, such as in an upcoming marriage. Red roses are a symbol of love, passion, and desire, while yellow roses convey friendship, happiness, and a caring spirit. Coral roses symbolize desire, while a white rose can reflect innocence, reverence, humility, and truth. Combining various colors of roses with white convey the thought of bonding and harmony. Red and white roses together symbolize unity.

**Ranunculus** is a delicate flower that conveys the symbol of "radiance." Giving this flower to someone would convey the expression, "you are radiant." Quite a fitting meaning, as I've used this particular flower throughout many designs in the book—it adds just the right amount of "radiance" to each arrangement.

**Succulents** have experienced a surge in popularity in recent years, providing a quirky touch to interiors with their striking and unusual appearance. They are believed to be a symbol of timeless love, with many brides choosing to incorporate them in their bouquets and centerpieces. In China, succulents are used as part of bringing feng shui into the home.

**Sunflowers** often give the expression of adoration. These majestic flowers adorn the center of many of my gardens.

**Tulips** have a special place in my heart, as they were in my wedding bouquet. Interestingly, tulips originated as a wildflower in Persia and in the 1500s they were primarily grown in Turkey. The Turkish loved the tulip due to the fact that it resembled the "tulbend," or turban, that they wore. By the late 1500s tulips were so rare that only the rich could afford them, and thus they became a status symbol. Tulips are associated with the declaration of love. Variegated tulips symbolize "beautiful eyes," "irresistible love" is conveyed by red tulips, while yellow tulips express "hopeless love with no chance of reconciliation." However, if red and yellow tulips are combined they offer a message of congratulation.

**Zinnias**, one of my favorites in my childhood garden, can express "I'm thinking of you, I miss you," such as in the absence of a friend. They can also convey lasting affection, constancy, and goodness.

PEONY

ROSE

RANUNCULUS

SUNFLOWER

TULIP

# Flower Types

Flowers can be classified into four basic types; line, mass, form, and accent (or fillers). Each of these types has its own function within an arrangement. Take a moment to familiarize yourself with and understand the function of these types, so if a particular flower that I have used is unavailable you can easily find a substitute.

**Line Flowers**

Line flowers are typically long and linear in shape. They can be identified by the blooms extending down their stem. They are commonly used to set the height, and sometimes the width, of an arrangement. They can also be used to give direction, such as in a horizontal arrangement.

DELPHINIUM

LILAC

DELPHINIUM

CARNATION

ASTIBILE

IRIS

**Form Flowers**

These flowers, while similar to line flowers, generally have their blooms located at the very top of the stem. They have a very distinctive shape, and are visually interesting, so they are helpful to add drama and a focal point.

TULIP

TIGER LILY

**Accent Flowers**

Sometimes called filler flowers, these generally have multi stems and are used to fill in between the main flowers in an arrangement, and to add texture and depth.

## Mass Flowers

Mass flowers generally have clusters of
flowers located on the end of the stem.
Typically they are used to create volume
and texture, but they can also be the focal
point in an arrangement.

RANUNCULUS

ROSE

POPPY

CHRYSANTHEMIUM

PEONY

GERANIUM

# Foliage Types

Foliage is usually used to provide a background for the flowers, but it is also useful to add texture or fullness to an arrangement. Variegated leaves also add color, while trailing stems are great to break up the straight lines of a container, or to extend a design widthwise. Remember you don't have to use the leaves that actually come with a flower—feel free to mix and match!

**TIP**

Obviously silk flowers have no scent, but if you want your arrangements to smell natural you can add a drop of essential oil to the base. Don't get it on the flower petals though, as the oil may stain them.

# Tools

You only need a few basic tools for arranging florals. I strongly suggest that you purchase quality tools. This will make your experience much more enjoyable and the tools will save you money by lasting you a lifetime.

**Wire cutters** This is one of those tools that you absolutely cannot do without, so do yourself a favor and invest in a very good pair. This will make cutting of the stems much easier and your hands will thank you in the long run. When choosing your wire cutters make sure they are comfortable with easy-to-grip handles. A spring in the handle will make cutting quick and easy, too. Make sure the blades open up wide enough to accommodate thicker stems.

**Serrated knife** Necessary to cut and shape foam—this type of knife will cut the foam quicker and easier than a plain blade.

**Scissors** These are another staple in your toolbox. Try to have two pairs, one that you can use for general purpose and another to cut fabric or ribbon. Don't use your scissors to

cut wire as this will create nicks that damage and dull the blades very quickly.

**Rubber mallet** A soft mallet is useful to tap foam down into containers, and roughly shape foam blocks. If you are arranging fresh flowers you can also use the mallet to crush the end of woody stems so they will take in more water. Some floral designers use a standard hammer, but I find the rubber mallet to have a much gentler effect on the foam.

**Tape measure** Useful if you need to be precise. Some designers always like to measure stems for length, but personally I save a bit of time and just estimate the length by eye.

**Pencil** An essential for marking, but also for making holes in the foam to accommodate thicker wires. You can also use an awl for this purpose.

# Wire and anchoring supplies

There are quite a few different type of wire and anchoring materials,
many of which are multi purpose. Most are inexpensive, so you can afford to keep a
good selection on hand.

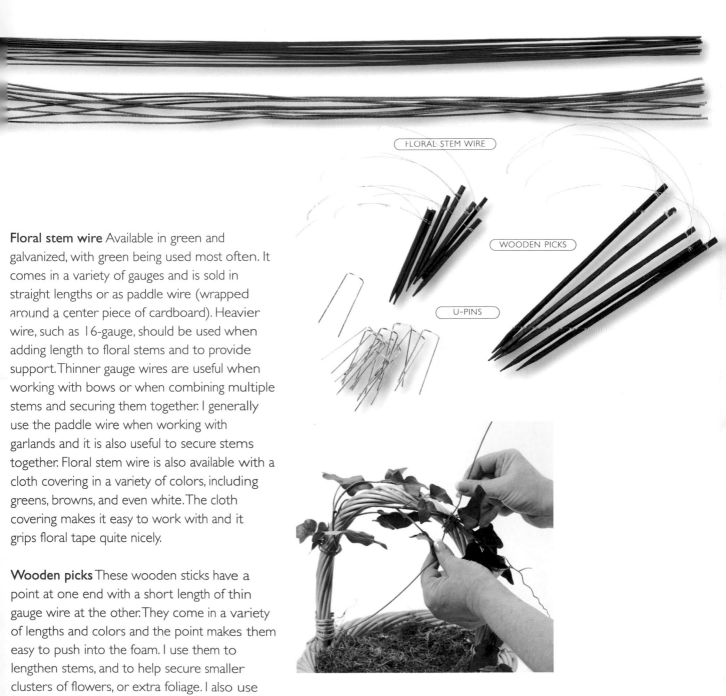

FLORAL STEM WIRE

WOODEN PICKS

U-PINS

**Floral stem wire** Available in green and
galvanized, with green being used most often. It
comes in a variety of gauges and is sold in
straight lengths or as paddle wire (wrapped
around a center piece of cardboard). Heavier
wire, such as 16-gauge, should be used when
adding length to floral stems and to provide
support. Thinner gauge wires are useful when
working with bows or when combining multiple
stems and securing them together. I generally
use the paddle wire when working with
garlands and it is also useful to secure stems
together. Floral stem wire is also available with a
cloth covering in a variety of colors, including
greens, browns, and even white. The cloth
covering makes it easy to work with and it
grips floral tape quite nicely.

**Wooden picks** These wooden sticks have a
point at one end with a short length of thin
gauge wire at the other. They come in a variety
of lengths and colors and the point makes them
easy to push into the foam. I use them to
lengthen stems, and to help secure smaller
clusters of flowers, or extra foliage. I also use
wooden picks to add faux fruits and vegetables
to my arrangements. When you attach any item
to a wooden pick cover the wire with floral
tape afterwards, to conceal it and achieve a
more natural appearance.

**Wooden bamboo skewers** Although I did not
use any skewers for the projects in this book,
they are particularly useful to provide additional
support when attaching multiple layers of
foam—simply insert one end through all the

layers of foam and cut off any excess. Skewers can also be inserted into the bottom of fruits and vegetables to secure such items into arrangements. Use natural colored skewers on real fruit so that the dye from the skewer does not stain them. These are nice to have handy, though I do not use them often.

**Floral U-pins** These pins are named for their "U" shape, but are also sometimes called "greening pins." They are ideal to secure a variety of materials, such as mosses and extra foliage. I also use them to secure flower stems or foliage temporarily in place as I design the arrangement, since they do very little damage to the foam base. For a more permanent grip, dip the ends of the pins into adhesive before inserting them into the foam, or insert two pins at opposite 45-degree angles.

FLORAL ADHESIVE CLAY

FLORAL TAPE

self-sealing, stretchable wrap to cover and conceal wires, picks and floral stems. It is waterproof and colorfast, and becomes tacky and sticks to itself when stretched—the sticky surface helps to hold wires and other materials in place. Choose a color of tape that will blend best with your design. I have also used floral tape to repair broken or damaged stems. As a note, there are many colors of green available—the olive-toned greens are more natural in appearance.

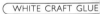

CLEAR TAPE

WHITE CRAFT GLUE

**Corsage pins/straight pins** Although we do not use corsage pins for the projects in this book, they are useful to secure items like ribbons and bows. Corsage pins and boutonniere pins have pearly ends, which can be both decorative and functional. These pins can also give a decorative touch to small flowers.

**Anchor pins** (not shown) These are small plastic disks that help to secure foam to the bottom of a container. I only use them when designing in opaque containers, such as terra cotta pots or vases.

**Floral tape** In a variety of colors from white to green, as well as various widths, floral tape is a

HOT GLUE MELTING PAN

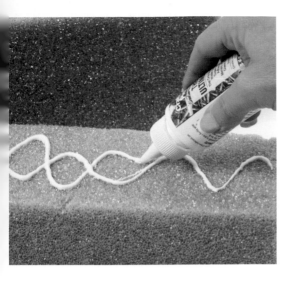

**Glue guns and glue sticks** These are used by a majority of floral designers. High heat glue creates a strong, fast bond and is an easy way to permanently secure florals and other items into the arrangement. Lo-Temp sticks are useful when the materials are heat sensitive, such as plastic foams. Make sure you use the appropriate glue for your heat gun.

**Floral adhesive clay** This is used to anchor plastic Styrofoam® (which is generally white), but will not work on the other types of foams used for dried or fresh flowers. It is also used to secure other items, such as candles in their holders. It comes in a roll and is very sticky.

**Hot glue pan** Similar to the glue guns except that the glue is melted in an electric pan, which comes in a variety of sizes. The glue is available in either pellets or chunks, which melt to a creamy, stringy consistency that reminds me of melted cheese. The advantage of using the pan is that you can dip the ends of the stems and then insert them directly into the arrangement.

**White craft glue** This is simply white tacky glue that dries clear and can also be used to secure stems. The big advantage of this glue is that it dries more slowly than the hot glue so there is time to adjust the stems before the glue sets. It is also great when you need to cover a large surface, such as when you are adhering moss to foam. It also makes a great alternative to hot glue when working with younger ones or those who might be more susceptible to burning themselves.

**TIP**

A glue gun will heat the glue to a temperature that will cause burning if the glue comes in contact with your skin. Have a bowl of cold water handy and if you burn yourself quickly dip the affected skin in the water to soothe it and help it to heal quickly. Using the hot glue pan instead may help to avoid burnt fingers.

GLUE GUN

HOT GLUE STICKS

# Foundation Materials

It's hard to build a house without a foundation, and the same is true with arranging florals, regardless of whether you are working with faux or fresh flowers. Choosing the right foundation will make your designing easier and more enjoyable. Knowing which material to use will also help you to create arrangements that are structurally sound and professional looking.

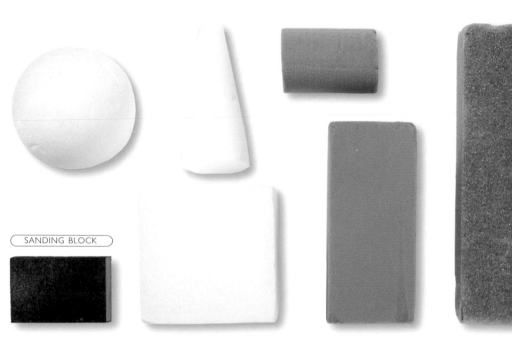

SANDING BLOCK

**TIP**

Consider the types of flowers and other materials you will be working with when choosing your foundation. For example, are the stems thick and heavy (and so need firm support), or are they rather light and delicate?

**Plasticfoam or Styrofoam®** This comes in both green and white and is available in many sizes and a wide variety of shapes such as cones, balls, flat sheets, rectangles, and cubes (see above). It is easy to cut and lightweight and can be painted if necessary with acrylic or spray paints. Note that some solvents will react and dissolve foam so be sure that the products you are using are compatible with it. Since plastic foam will not absorb water, it is a good choice if your arrangement is to be placed outdoors. Plastic foam is also suitable for materials that are glued or attached with U-pins, and is ideal for thicker stems and heavier arrangements. It isn't such a good option for delicate dried items unless you secure them onto wooden picks first. Floral clay will work on this type of foam.

**Dried silk foam** Sold in bricks in colors such as gray, brown, and green, this is very lightweight, delicate material so it is not a good choice if your arrangement is heavy. It will shatter if large,

thick stems are inserted. Use glue tape, wire, or hot glue to anchor this foam in arrangements, since floral clay will not stick to it.

**Fresh floral foam** This is a necessity if you are working with fresh flowers. It should be soaked in water first to hydrate it and to prepare it for fresh stems—simply fill a sink or deep bowl with water and place the foam inside, then leave it to fully absorb the water. While the arrangements in this book fool the eye and look fresh they are not, so we did not use this type of foam. However, once you have learned a few basic skills, you may want to try arranging fresh flowers using this foam as a base.

**River rocks** These give a natural and organic flair to your base. They are used in a similar way to the glass marbles.

**Mosses** There are several different types of real moss available that are all idea for faux floral

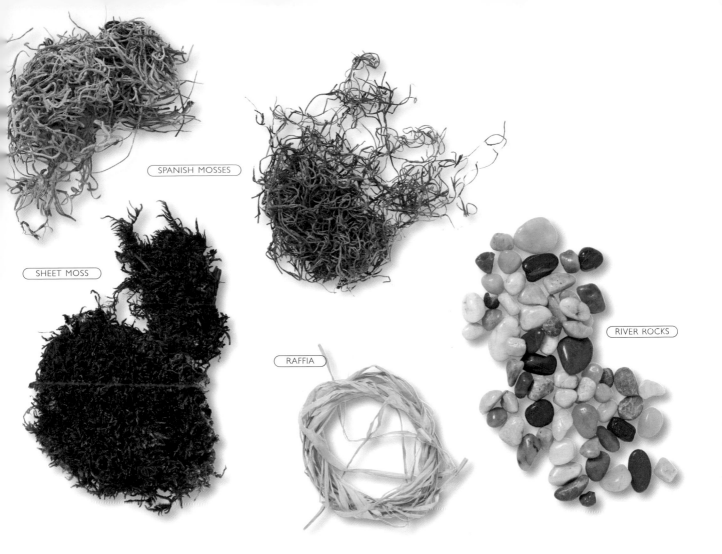

SPANISH MOSSES

SHEET MOSS

RAFFIA

RIVER ROCKS

arrangements. Moss is great to conceal the support foams and to give your arrangements a natural, fresh-from-the-garden look.

**Glass marbles** For a fresh, just-picked look, I like to anchor floral stems in glass marbles. They are easy to use; simply pour a small amount into the container, arrange the flowers and add a few more marbles if necessary. The weight of the glass secures the stems in place and gives an elegant effect. The marbles come in a variety of shapes, colors, and sizes. Typically I use smaller marbles for more delicate arrangements and larger marbles for those that are taller and contain heavier floral stems. Marbles are also a great choice for fresh flower arranging.

**Acrylic Water** This is a two-part resin-based material that simulates the look of water in the bottom of an arrangement and can be used alone or with glass marbles or river rocks. The resin will set, but this can take anything from a few minutes to several hours—check the manufacturer's instructions. Allow the arrangement to set on a level surface in a warm area. This will help the resin to cure more quickly. Acrylic water is usually permanent, but there are some types that are reusable. Please check the package carefully.

ACRYLIC WATER

GLASS MARBLES

# Containers

As you can see in the photo, containers come in a variety of shapes, colors, and sizes. Containers compliment the look of your design and set the tone for the finished arrangement. Selection of the perfect container is important, but don't stress about it!

The perfect container need not be expensive to achieve the right showcase for your work—maybe it is just an interesting shape. Have a look around your home, as you may already own just the right thing! Inexpensive glass containers are readily available and come in a variety of sizes—they are a great choice when you are simulating the look of freshly picked flowers. Be creative and think about things you may already have, such as that old terra cotta pot with sentimental value, or maybe an old drawer that belonged to a grandmother. Using something with a sentimental value will add meaning to your arrangement.

When choosing a container, it is important give attention to the size and shape of the finished arrangement, and where you will be placing it. Also consider the style of décor in the area. Contemporary containers are sleek and simple, traditional ones are refined and generally made from metal or glass, country containers are durable and feature a more natural organic feel. Don't just think of traditional vases—terra cotta pots, canning jars, and baskets can all be good choices for an unusual arrangement. A word of caution, though: when selecting a container for use in projects that require acrylic water, make sure that the container is watertight!

# Techniques

The techniques shown here are used again and again across most of the projects. A few additional special techniques are shown in the relevant projects.

## Cutting stems

Cut stems off at an angle. This creates a point at the end and makes it easier to push the flower into the foam. Sometimes the stems can be quite tough, so use wire cutters to ensure you get a clean finish at the end of each one.

**TIP**

If you need to thicken up a stem, fold floral stem wire in half and bind the doubled-up section to the stem with florist's tape.

## Cutting single blooms from bush

Rather than buying several single stems, often it is less expensive to purchase a bush of flowers and simply cut the stems apart at the base. You can use these single stems to create a more pleasing arrangement or spread them around an arrangement to make best use of the material. Lengthen the stems if necessary for taller arrangements.

## Lengthening a stem

1 To lengthen a stem that is too short, simply use an extra stem of around the same thickness.
2 Place the extra stem next to the flower stem and wrap together with floral tape to secure.

## Trimming extra flowers

**1** Trim off any extra or unwanted flowers or leaves. This helps to prevent unnecessary bulk inside the container. Keep the extra flower stems and leaves for future use—you can lengthen the stem if you need to.

**2** If necessary, turn the stem around to trim off the excess stalk from the other side to get a neat finish.

**TIP**

Sometimes stems of silk flowers have indentations at intervals along the length. You don't have to trim the length at these stages, but if you do it will be easier to cut here where the stem is a bit thinner.

## Adding a leaf to a stem

**1** Trim off any excess material from the base of the leaf.

**2** Add a length of floral wire to the base of the leaf.

**3** Secure the leaf in place by wrapping with floral tape.

**4** Place the wired leaf against the stem and wrap with floral tape securing it into position.

continued next page

## Spreading out material

**1** Sprays of berries can be removed and made into single clusters by removing individual berry clusters from the branch.

**2** Arrange one or two clusters at the top of a wood pick. Wrap wire around the clusters to secure to the pick.

**3** Wrap the entire pick stem with floral tape to hide the wires. Trim off any excess material to refine the shape of the spray.

## Covering foam with moss

**1** Secure moss to the foam by pressing U-pins into the foam.

**2** To camouflage the pin, add a daub of glue to the top.

**3** Apply a small patch of moss over the glue to conceal the U-pin.

1

2

## Cutting foam/oasis

**1** Foam can easily be cut and sized to fit your container. Mark the size roughly on the foam. Use a serrated knife to cut the foam, for a cleaner cut.

**2** Saw backward and forward gently to make the cutting easier. To smooth the edges, simply rub with sandpaper. It isn't necessary to be perfect when cutting foam—you can fill in with smaller pieces and cover with moss.

1

2

3

## Using acrylic water

**1** Follow the manufacturer's safety instructions and work in a well-ventilated area. Combine both bottles in a disposable cup or bowl.

**2** Stir the mixture together well, making sure that it is thoroughly mixed. (This takes about one minute.)

**3** Gently pour the acrylic water into the vase, being careful not to drip it down the sides. If you do happen to get a drop on the side, immediately wipe with a paper towel until all the residue has been removed.

# Rescue Remedies

Ooops—I did that wrong! Is that what you're thinking? Don't worry, it's not too late.
We've all done it: cut that stem too short; snipped off a flower or leaf we actually needed.
Generally there isn't a problem we can't fix and hide. Here are some tips I've
put together to help save those little goofs.

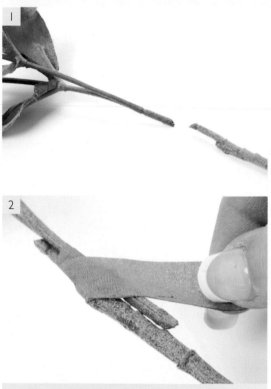

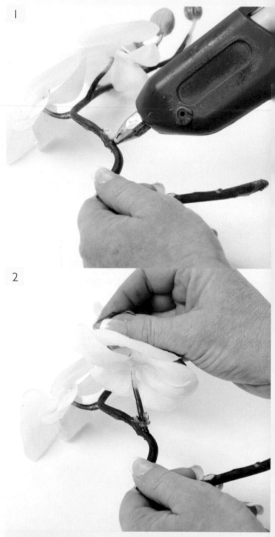

### Replacing the stem
1 If you have cut a stem too short, you can replace the end. Overlap the ends slightly.
2 Secure the stems together with floral tape.

### Replacing a flower
1 If you cut off a flower by mistake, it can be replaced with a daub of glue from the glue gun.
2 Touch the tip of the flower stalk to the glue and hold in place until it cools.

### Trimming fraying leaves or petals
Sometimes general wear and tear will get the better of your silk flowers and the edges of petals or leaves will start to fray. To solve this problem simply trim around the edges with a sharp pair of scissors to make them as good as new.

### Repairing a drooping petal
1 Sometimes a petal will droop down away from the others. Even in nature this happens, but if you find it unsightly, simply add a dab of hot glue to the area.

2 Gently press the petal back into place and hold for a second until it is set.

### Repairing flock stems
1 Some stems have furry flocking on them to make them appear more realistic. However, the problem is that sometimes this rubs off, leaving part of the stem bare and unsightly.
2 To disguise the damage, simply wrap the entire stem in floral tape.
3 The finished stem looks good as new.

# Design Elements

Understanding the elements of design will help make floral arranging easy and more enjoyable. Knowing a few key principals will help you when selecting flowers, foliage, and containers for your finished arrangement and give it visual appeal. Let's discuss a few of these key principals briefly:

PROPORTION

**Visual balance** is how the arrangement appears. A balanced arrangement is pleasing to the eye.

**Symmetrical** or designs that are the same on both sides of the arrangement will give a more formal look.

**Asymmetrical** designs, when things are not the same or those that shift the focal point to either side of the centerline, will appear less formal. Balance is created in asymmetrical designs by varying the size, shape, and colors in the arrangement. You will notice that many of the Fresh from the Garden designs featured later in the book have an asymmetrical design to them and thus they appear less formal.

**Harmony** is achieved when all the components blend together well and form a visually appealing arrangement. You can achieve harmony with the use of similar materials or using petals and leaves of the same color, for example.

HARMONY

**Proportion** refers to the relationship in size between the flowers, foliage, or the container. This is an important aspect to consider when creating your designs—and also keep in mind the relationship the finished arrangement will have to its surroundings.

## Color

Choosing colors is the most important element of the design process. There are numerous ways to combine color, and playing with color is fun! It is usually best to have one focal color and use other colors to support it. Dark, bright and intense colors work best when located towards the center of your design. Light colors will brighten the edges of the design. Warm colors are more dominant, while cool colors are restful and will tend to blend into the background. Keep in mind, too, that colors change slightly with varying light. Candlelight will make cool colors seem to fade and disappear and make bright colors appear stronger. Consider the color of the container as well, and repeat that in the floral design to achieve balance.

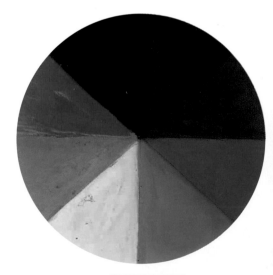

COLOR WHEEL

## Monochromatic

These designs are all one color. Interest is created by varying the shade or tint of the flower along with a variety of different sizes of the flowers, and the texture.

## Analogous

This design uses colors that are next to each other on the color wheel.

## Triadic

A triadic arrangement uses three colors that are the same distance apart on the color wheel.

## Complementary

Complementary designs use colors opposite on the color wheel.

## Split complementary

This color scheme uses a main color along with two colors on either side of the color wheel.

MONOCHROMATIC

ANALOGOUS

COMPLEMENTARY

TRIADIC

SPLIT COMPLEMENTARY

# Shape

There are many shape choices, making the design process always fresh and fun. Let's take a look at some of the most common.

**Fan** arrangements, also called a triangular arrangement, tend to be viewed from one side. The shape of this design tends to give off a more formal feel.

**Linear or vertical designs** have very distinct tall lines and are often featured in designs that are more natural in appearance, like flowers growing in a garden. These designs tend to be very dramatic.

**Horizontal** arrangements are often used as table centerpieces. They are generally low in height and have long lines that run parallel to the surface on which they sit. Use line flowers to establish the width of the display.

LINEAR OR VERTICAL

FAN

HORIZONTAL

**Round** designs are classic. These designs are beautiful from all sides because their flowers radiate from a center focal point. This design is a good choice when you want to create contemporary or traditional designs.

**Topiaries** feature a slender stem, of sticks or rods, that supports a cluster of flowers at the top. There are topiary forms that can be purchased or, as you will see in a later project, you can create your own very simply.

TOPIARY

ROUND

## Textures

**Textures** create visual interest and can be either physical (soft, rough, coarse, etc.) or visual (shiny or dull). Using textures that are similar helps to create harmony and they are a vital component when working in monochromatic designs. Texture can also give the design a feminine feel by being delicate and light, or a more masculine feel by using rough or matte materials.

**Movement, rhythm, and repetition** should be considered when designing. Rhythm helps the materials visually flow and brings harmony to the arrangement. You can create rhythm and repetition by repeating a certain element throughout the design. Personally I create in odd numbers—using three, five, or seven sets of the same flower in a design. This is also where I play with textures to create movement and visual interest. I like to add lots of movement in my designs, helping the eye travel visually throughout the arrangement in a pleasing way. It also helps to keep the designs looking fresh and informal.

# Taking Care of Florals

With a little care your flower arrangements can look their best for a long time to come. Give careful consideration to their position—do not display your arrangements in direct sunlight to prevent fading and damage.

**TIP**

If you have an arrangement that you really love that is looking a bit sad and worn out, try gently removing some of the tattered florals and replace them with new ones.

There are sprays for cleaning flowers available on the market. Simply follow the manufacturer's directions to obtain the best results.

You can also dust your arrangements using a can of compressed air, or use your hairdryer on a "no-heat" setting. If you change arrangements regularly, keep unused flowers safe by wrapping them in a plastic sack and placing them in a cool, dry, dark place.

You can also store your leftover stems for future use. Clear plastic storage containers are excellent choices for storing flowers by color or type and will keep them in good condition for future projects.

# CHAPTER 1

# Bright & Informal

How wonderful it is to receive a beautiful bunch
of fresh flowers or a vibrantly green plant to liven up your home.
In this chapter we create the look of
fresh flowers and plants, but with a twist!
These botanicals and greenery will last a lifetime,
so now you have the best of both worlds: the crispness
of fresh blooms and plants and a display that will
delight you for many years to come.

# Lilac Bouquet

This fresh and simple bouquet of lilacs is very simple to create, making it ideal to display on a coffee table, nightstand, or anywhere you want a breath of fresh air. Lilac blooms are quite full so they create a good mass of color and great texture, which means additional flowers are not really needed. Try adding a drop of lilac essential oils to give your room a fresh-from-the-garden fragrance.

## FLORALS
- 1 lilac bush or 7 stems of full white lilac blooms
- 4 stems of partially budded white lilac

## OTHER MATERIALS
- Length of fabric covered wire
- Length of raffia tape
- Pack of clear acrylic water
- Medium-size glass vase

## TIP
If you drip acrylic water down the side of your glass vase as you pour, wipe it off straight away using a clean section of paper towel each time you wipe.

1 Mix the acrylic water according to the manufacturer's directions and pour it into the vase, trying not to drip it down the sides.

2 Cut individual stems from your bush of lilac, as described on page 26. Arrange the stems into an attractive bunch. Trim the ends of each stem to the same length.

3 Twist a length of fabric-covered wire several times around the stems to hold them securely in shape. Twist the ends of wire together and fold them back around the bunch.

4 Bind the stems with raffia to hide the wire and tie the ends into an attractive bow. Place the bouquet into the vase. Place the vase on a flat surface and allow acrylic water to set for 24 hours.

# Tied Iris Bouquet

This stunning, yet simple, arrangement features the beauty of the iris, allowing its splashes of purple color to take center stage. Think of unusual materials to encase the stems, such as ribbon, raffia, or fabric, to name but a few. In this case, however, the bouquet of stems was wrapped in a single leaf in keeping with the simple but elegant design.

## FLORALS
- 2 iris bushes or 14 stems of purple iris
- Large leaf

## OTHER MATERIALS
- Length of fabric-covered wire
- Glue gun
- Pack of acrylic water
- Wide glass vase

## NOTE
The design is not meant to stand exactly upright but to rest on the sides of the glass vase.

1 Set the vase onto a flat surface. Mix the acrylic water as described on page 29 and add it to the vase. Arrange the irises into an attractive bunch and bind in place with a length of fabric-covered wire.

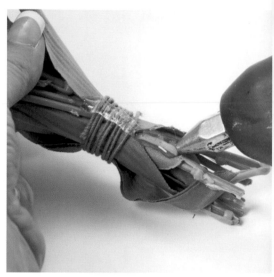

2 Apply hot glue in small dots around the base of the iris stems with the glue gun. (Be cautious—glue is hot and will burn your skin if you come in contact.)

3 Wrap the leaf around the stems leaving approximately ¾ in. (18 mm) extending beyond the stems. Secure in the seam with a dot of hot glue. Hold in place until glue has set.

4 Fold the bottom edge of the leaf inward to finish the bottom of the bouquet. Secure with hot glue. Place the bouquet into the vase and leave the acrylic water to set, following the manufacturer's instructions.

# Rosebud Garden

A crystal vase can add a touch of class to any arrangement. Perhaps you have a piece of heirloom crystal that has been handed down to you—why not make it the center of attention with this romantic arrangement of pink rosebuds and delicate rock cress? The clear glass marbles will hold the flowers in place without damaging the vase.

**FLORALS**
- 12 pink rosebuds
- 1 bush of rock cress, cut into single stems

**OTHER MATERIALS**
- Clear glass marbles
- Tall glass or crystal vase

1 Cut five rose stems to 9 in. (22.5 cm), six stems to 12 in. (30 cm) and one stem to 14 in. (35 cm).

2 Place the longest rose in the center. Place the shorter roses around the center rose.

3 Add the medium length roses between the long and short to fill creating an open arrangement. Trim any excess leaves away.

4 Working around the design, add sprays of rock cress for a touch of delicate texture.

# Concrete Pots

The graphic shapes and contemporary look of these little pots contrasts well with the striking forms of the faux succulents, while the addition of a little moss gives a professional look. Display them in a group, or dot them around your home, for a stylish and contemporary botanical feature.

1 Cut a piece of foam to fit inside the pot—it does not need to be too neat, but the foam should fit snugly inside the pot and sit about 3/8 in (1 cm) below the rim.

2 Push the foam into the pot, shaving off small slivers if necessary to fit it in.

3 Tear a small piece of moss from the sheet and put on top of the pot. It should look a little rough round the edges, and trail over the edge a little in places.

4 Push a succulent through the moss and into the foam so that it sits into the moss slightly. If the succulent you are using has a very long stem you may need to trim it.

# Wildflower Medley

This arrangement particularly reminds me of my garden as a child, as these were the flowers that I always planted and nurtured. I recall the birds singing, the bees buzzing, as I gazed at the beautiful arrays of sunny yellow. When arranging wildflowers, select your main flower color, then chose other flowers that pick up on different color shades within the main blooms.

## FLORALS

- 4 stems of yellow/orange cosmos
- 1 yellow snapdragon
- 1 neutral snapdragon
- 1 bush mini yellow daisy cut into individual stems
- 2 small yellow ranunculus blooms
- 3 sprigs of white berries

## OTHER MATERIALS

- Clear glass marbles
- Glass vase

## TIP

This arrangement is designed to be light and airy, not bunched together in a tight arrangement. It is okay if some of the flowers fall to one side as this happens in nature also.

**1** Look at the flowers together and work out the dominant color and texture that will form the basis of your arrangement.

**2** The first flowers you place are to establish the overall height and the main color focus of your arrangement.

**3** Add the contrast colors in next, placing the blooms to highlight all the different shades within the other flowers.

**4** Finally fill in any gaps with the ranunculus and the berry sprays.

# Autumn Sunflowers

As the air in autumn turns crisp, the leaves begin changing colors from green to vibrantly rich shades of russet and gold. Sunflowers compliment autumn shades with their dramatic bold blooms—combine them with some bright colored berries for a festive and seasonal arrangement.

## FLORALS
- I sunflower bush, cut into individual stems
- I bells of Ireland bush, cut into individual stems
- Several sprigs of large berries
- Several sprigs of small berries
- Several stems of Autumn-color leaves

## OTHER MATERIALS
- Tall glass vase
- 5 large leaves

I Trim off any excess leaves from the sunflowers and set aside. Tidy up the stem, cutting off any excess material.

2 Create the basic shape of the arrangement with the sunflowers, adjusting them into a pleasing symmetrical shape.

3 Arrange the berries and foliage around the design to fill in any gaps between the sunflowers and add movement and interest to the basic shape.

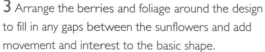

4 Slide large leaves down the side of the vase to hide the stems. Repeat with additional leaves all the way around until the vase has been completely lined.

# Symphony in Pink

A variety of different ranunculus blooms, all in shades of harmonious pink, provide the basis for this display. Sprays of curving bells and deep pink and white flowers lend a delicate note to the overall design. If any of the flowers used are not available in your area, feel free to substitute something similar.

## FLORALS
- 7 stems of large, deep pink ranunculus blooms
- 3 stems of small dark pink ranunculus blooms cut from a bush
- 2 stems of small medium pink ranunculus blooms cut from a bush
- 2 stems of small light pink ranunculus blooms cut from a bush
- 4 sprays of curving white flowers of your choice
- I bush of deep pink and white flowers, cut into individual sprays
- 4 sprays of leaves
- I trailing stem of leaves cut from a bush

## OTHER MATERIALS
- Block of foam
- Serrated knife
- Rubber mallet (optional)
- Wooden picks
- Medium-size ceramic vase

1 Cut the block of foam roughly to shape with the knife and tap it down gently into the vase with the mallet.

2 Arrange the deep pink ranunculus flowers creating a curving dome shape over the top of the vase.

3 Fill in the bigger gaps between the large blooms with the small ranunculus blooms, trying to keep the placement balanced around the arrangement.

4 Add a few curving white sprays at intervals, giving movement and extra visual interest to the design.

**5** Add sprays of pink and white flowers around the edges. If necessary tape sprays of foliage to wooden picks, and add to the arrangement creating additional texture.

**6** Attach the trailing stem to a wooden pick and tuck the end in at the base on one side, curve the foliage around and tuck the other end into the top of the vase on the other side, allowing it to hang on a flower stem. You may choose to secure with a daub of hot glue.

# Meadow Flowers

I imagine walking through a meadow on a warm sunny day, enjoying the fresh air and collecting flowers to create this pretty arrangement. Blue lilacs are the focus and are accented by a variety of other colorful blooms. The stems are concealed with moss, which has been placed into the vase before the arranging begins. Soften the look by adding a sprig of trailing vine to the front.

## FLORALS
- 2 stems of blue lilac
- 3 stems of pink tiger lilies
- I white and pink peony
- I large peony bud
- 2 small peony buds
- 3 stems of astibile
- Various berry stems
- 3 stems of bells of Ireland
- 2 stems of white arching flowers
- I trailing foliage stem

## OTHER MATERIALS
- Sheet moss
- Glue gun
- Tall glass vase

## TIP
If the colors I have used here do not complement your décor, you can simply substitute different color flowers.

1 Begin by lining the glass vase with patches of sheet moss—it does not have to be one large piece. Fill in any gaps with smaller pieces, as these will not show after the arrangement is complete.

2 Create the bouquet of flowers in your hand, arranging them in a pleasing matter. Carefully place the bouquet in the vase, being careful not to disturb the moss. Adjust the stems if necessary.

3 Push one end of the trailing foliage stem in among the flowers on one side then loop it across the front of the vase, then tuck the end in among the flowers to secure.

4 For a fresh and natural look, pull the stems up slightly to open out the bouquet. For a slightly more formal appeal, press the stems a little tighter inside the base.

# Shades of Green

Sticking to faux succulents of a similar color will give your display a calm, elegant feel and adding a few pretty shells and gravel gives additional interest. Use trailing plants around the edge of the bowl so that they tumble over the edge, and finish with a few handfuls of gravel.

## FLORALS
- Selection of large faux succulents in shades of green such as aeonium, senecio radicans, aloe, and sedum

## OTHER MATERIALS
- Large metal bowl
- Block of Styrofoam®
- Serrated knife
- Floral adhesive clay
- Gravel
- Scissors or wire cutters
- Large shells

1 Cut the foam to sit inside the bowl, using several pieces if necessary and adding small pieces of foam around the edges to fill gaps. Don't worry about it being neat. Use floral adhesive clay to hold the foam in place.

2 Add handfuls of gravel over the foam to form an even layer, spreading it around the bowl neatly.

3 Arrange the succulents, trimming the stems if they are very long until you are happy with the placing of each one. Use trailing succulents around the edge of the bowl.

4 Add a few shells between the succulents for extra decoration.

CHAPTER 2

# Formal Displays

In this chapter, you'll find arrangements that are
designed to make a stunning visual impact. This doesn't mean
they are difficult to create—far from it—but they are
dramatic or unusual in some way. Some of them
may little bit more time to get just right. Once completed
though, these are the arrangements that will be
the envy of your friends!

# Triple Tulips

Tiny arrangements like these are simply stunning grouped in a row on a windowsill or on a buffet. Simple and quick to create they are also ideal for table decorations, either arranged down the center or at individual place settings. Personally, I believe these are an ideal addition to decorate your table for an afternoon tea party.

**FLORALS**
- 3 tulips
- 9 small sprays of white flowers
- 3 sprays of leaves

**OTHER MATERIALS**
- 3 small glass bowls
- Clear glass marbles

1 Remove all the small leaves from the sprays of white flowers.

2 Attach three sprays of white flowers to a leaf stem using floral tape.

3 Cut a tulip stem quite short and tape it to the flower and leaf spray.

4 Add glass marbles to the bowls and push one stem down into each of them.

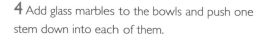

# Vintage Teacups

Pretty teacups in pastel colors make an unusual planter idea for mini succulents. These are very quick and easy to assemble and would make a lovely centerpiece for a dinner table. Why not collect vintage teacups from thrift stores or yard sales, plant them up with a faux succulent, and give to guests as wedding or party favors?

## FLORALS
- Selection of faux succulents such as sedum, echeveria, and sempervivum

## OTHER MATERIALS
- Teacups in pretty colors
- Small blocks of Styrofoam®
- Serrated knife
- Fine gravel
- Scissors or wire cutters

**1** Cut the foam to fit roughly inside the cup, shaving off sections as necessary. It does not need to be too neat.

**2** Push the foam inside the cup, trimming away any excess so that the foam sits snugly inside the cup with the surface about 3/8 in (1 cm) below the rim.

**3** Add a small handful of gravel to the cup, spreading it out evenly and filling any gaps between the foam and the cup.

**4** Check that the stem of the succulent is not taller than the cup. If it is then trim it a little. Push the stem in to the foam so that the base of the succulent sits on the gravel.

# Peony Cube

A moss-lined glass cube vase holds a delightful display of frilly white and pink peonies, white spray flowers and white berries. This is a really simple arrangement to create, but is an ideal display for any occasion or when a small space needs just a hint of color.

## FLORALS
- 3 peonies
- 3 sprays of berries
- 3 sprays of white flowers

## OTHER MATERIALS
- Small block of Styrofoam®
- Floral U-pins
- Sheet of moss
- Small square glass vase

## TIP
When lining a glass container with sheet moss, secure the moss to the top edge of the vase with a little glue so it does not fall down when you add the flowers.

**1** Cut a block of foam a little smaller than the square vase and wrap it around with a piece of sheet moss.

**2** Place the wrapped foam in the vase and trim another piece of sheet moss to cover the top. Attach with U-pins, then cover the U-pins with moss, if necessary, to conceal them.

**3** Push the first peony firmly into the foam to establish the main point of the design.

**4** Add the other two peonies towards the back on each side.

**5** Add sprays of berries around the peonies.

**6** Fill in any gaps around the design with the white spray flowers.

# Bowl of White Poppies

Using white poppies instead of the normal brightly colored ones creates a more contemporary look that will complement any décor. If you prefer to use red poppies, omit the other white flowers and replace them with extra foliage, more poppies, or colored berries.

## FLORALS
- 6 stems of white poppies
- 2 stems of white ranunculus
- 4 stems of astibile
- 3 stems of any arching white flower

## OTHER MATERIALS
- 6 in. (15 cm) Styrofoam® ball
- Serrated knife
- Sheet moss
- Floral U-pins
- Glue gun
- Green ceramic dish or bowl of choice

**1** Prepare a Styrofoam® base as described in steps 1–2 on page 86. Attach the base with hot glue to the bowl. Add the first three poppies establishing the height of the arrangement.

**2** Cut the remaining poppies quite short and add them and the ranunculus stems to make a curving arch arrangement.

**3** Add the curving white flowers on either side and at the front to bring movement to the design.

**4** Introduce some astibile stems to fill in any gaps in the arrangement and to add texture.

# Orchid Accent

Orchids are often displayed growing from a bulb that is set in a clear glass bowl. Unfortunately the real flowers can often be rather difficult to grow and maintain successfully, so get the same effect without the stress by using a real bulb and a faux flower.

**FLORALS**
- 1 stem of orchid
- Spare long leaves
- 1 large flower bulb (an amaryllis bulb works well)

**OTHER MATERIALS**
- Floral tape
- Sharp knife
- Glue gun
- River rocks
- Small square glass vase

**1** Arrange the spare leaves on the orchid stem and secure them in place with floral tape.

**2** Hollow out the center of the flower bulb with a sharp knife, being careful not to cut too large a hole in the top.

**3** Cut the flower stem to the right length, add hot glue to the hole in the bulb and push the end of the stem carefully deep into the top of the bulb. Wipe off any excess glue that oozes out.

**4** Place a large dab of hot glue in the base of the glass vase. Push the bulb down into the glue and leave to set. Add a handful of colored river rocks around the bulb as desired.

# Iris Fountain

Limiting the selection of flowers, in combination with a dramatic vertical design, can create an arrangement that has real visual impact. Notice how the combination of the two types of flowers in complementary colors has added drama to this design.

### FLORALS
- 2 open-flower stems of iris
- 3 partially open stems of iris
- 3 iris buds
- 8 yellow rosebuds
- Several sprays of white flowers

### OTHER MATERIALS
- Glass vase

**1** Gather all the iris flowers together and drop into the center of your vase to set the full height of the arrangement. Adjust the height if necessary to coordinate with your container or suit your personal taste.

**2** Cut the stems of the rosebuds, if necessary, so that the buds lie just on the edge of the vase. Place the rosebuds around the entire perimeter of the design.

**3** Add additional sprays of white flowers at intervals around the arrangement to add movement and fill the design.

**4** Finally, tweak the iris blooms, if necessary, so that they sit centrally in the design.

# Shades of Winter

The rounded shapes of viburnum flowers lend themselves to creating this spherical arrangement of blooms in soft shades of white and pastel green. Additional interest comes from the different textures and shapes of the ranunculus and the berry sprigs.

## FLORALS
- 1 bush of white viburnum flowers, cut into single stems
- 1 bush of white ranunculus, cut into single stems
- Sprigs of white berries
- 1 stem of astibile cut into sprays

## OTHER MATERIALS
- Clear glass marbles
- Pack of clear acrylic water
- Glass bowl

## TIP
This arrangement would look equally effective created in gently toning shades of the same color.

1 Mix the acrylic water according to the manufacturer's instructions. Half-fill the base of the bowl with marbles and acrylic water.

2 Create a rounded ball of flowers with the viburnum flowers.

3 Add ranunculus where desired and the white berries for texture.

4 Place sprays of astibile around the ball of flowers to add interest and movement to the design.

# Terrarium Display

This elegant terrarium will bring a touch of class to any room. Choose three large succulents in contrasting colors and shapes to create real interest, add dried moss and compost, and no one will ever guess that your terrarium is faux.

## FLORALS
- 3 medium faux succulents such as echeveria, sedum, and sempervivum

## OTHER MATERIALS
- Large open necked glass jar or vase
- Compost
- Gravel
- Sheet moss
- Clumps of dried moss
- Scissors or wire cutters
- Pebbles, stones, or pinecones

1 Add a few handfuls of compost to the bottom of the jar—you will need a layer about 1¼ in (3cm) thick.

2 Spread the compost out to form an even layer across the base of the jar and press the surface down firmly with the back of your hand.

3 Carefully add handfuls of gravel over the compost, making sure that the two don't mix—they should form neat layers.

4 Tear a rough circle of dried sheet moss to fit over the gravel. Put it into the jar, tucking the edges in neatly.

continued next page

**5** Take the tallest succulent and push it through the moss towards the back of the jar. Trim the stem if necessary, so that the succulent sits on the surface of the moss.

**6** Push the remaining two succulents in place, to make a nice arrangement.

**7** Add a few stones, pieces of dried moss, or pinecones to finish off the terrarium.

**8** Clean up the inside of the jar, using a paintbrush to remove any specks of compost or moss.

# Big and Bold

This striking planter uses large, bold shapes and colors to create a real centerpiece ideal for a mantle or table. Choose faux succulents in a range of colors and textures, planted in a rough concrete planter to really highlight the shape of the plants.

**FLORALS**
- Large faux succulents echeveria, Californian bud, sedum, purple sedum, and kalanchoe

**OTHER MATERIALS**
- Concrete trough
- Blocks of Styrofoam®
- Serrated knife
- Decorative glass pieces
- Scissors or wire cutters

1 Shape one of the foam blocks to fit into one end of the trough, so the surface of the foam is at least ⅝in (1.5cm) below the rim of the trough. Cut another block to fit inside the other end of the trough, so that both blocks fit snugly.

2 Pour the glass pieces into the trough, covering the foam completely. Spread them out to form an even layer.

3 Start to push the succulents in to the foam, using the flatter ones at the ends of the trough.

4 Continue to push the stems of the succulents into the foam, building up the middle section with taller plants until you are happy with the arrangement.

# Orchid Bowl

With these exotic white orchids you only need one single flower stem, in a simple arrangement with a few leaves, to make the most wonderful display. The clear acrylic water will hold the arrangement firmly in place and makes it look really lifelike.

## FLORALS

- 1 stem of Phalaenopsis or moth orchid
- 2–3 stems of heart-shaped leaves

## OTHER MATERIALS

- Tape (any color)
- Glue gun
- Pack of clear acrylic water
- Globe-shape glass vase

**1** Wrap the stem around the outside of your bowl to estimate the length of stem required. Remove any extra flower stalks that will be too low and cut the stem to the correct length. If your flower stem did not come with leaves, choose any medium to large heart-shape leaf.

**2** If your stem is too top-heavy to stand up in the bowl, use some marbles in the base to hold it in position. Place strips of tape across the top of the bowl in a criss-cross pattern to support your flowers while the acrylic water sets.

**3** Place the main flower stem in the vase so it drapes nicely over the edge, allowing it to rest against the tape to keep it in position so it does not move.

**4** When you are happy with the position of the flower, add two or three leaf stems to balance the arrangement.

**5** Mix clear acrylic water as per the manufacturer's instructions. Pour it into the vase, then leave to set for at least 24 hours on a level surface.

**6** When the acrylic water has fully set, carefully remove the tape from the top of the vase.

# Magnolia Cascade

This classic triangular shaped design of white flowers is simple but sophisticated and will lend a sleek contemporary look to your décor. The shape is created in easy stages, working from high to low—stand back at intervals to assess the overall effect as you work.

**FLORALS**
- 6 magnolia stems

**OTHER MATERIALS**
- Clear glass marbles
- Medium-size glass vase
- Glue gun

**TIP**

Don't worry about gluing material to your vase. The glue will hold items in place only temporarily and you can pull them away without harming the vase, should you want to make a change to the display later.

**1** Add glass marbles to the vase until it is half full. Cut some of the magnolia stems shorter and trim off any leaves that are near the base of the stem.

**2** Arrange the longest stem of magnolia to create the highest point of the design.

**3** Use the shorter stems to create the low area of the design. Fill in the cascade shape with the remaining flowers.

**4** To keep the blooms just where you want them, you can add a dab of glue to the edge of the vase and use it to secure a leaf or stem in place.

# Beside the Sea

These charming terrariums use wide rimmed glass goblets, and a selection of small-scale succulents. Cut small sections from larger faux plants if you can't get hold of small plants. Adding a layer of compost, although not needed for practical reasons, adds a touch of authenticity to the display.

**FLORALS**

- A few small faux succulents such as echeveria, sedum hispanicum, pachyveria, and aeonium

**OTHER MATERIALS**

- Selection of glass goblets, or vases with wide necks
- Handful of compost
- Decorative sand
- Fine gravel
- Pretty pebbles or stones
- Tiny shells
- Scissors or wire cutters

1 Clean the glass goblets and vases and dry thoroughly. Add a small handful of compost to the bottom of the glass and spread it out evenly to a thickness of about $^7/_8$ in (2cm).

2 Pour sand over the compost, making sure that it doesn't mix with the compost. Make an even layer about $^5/_8$ in (1.5cm) thick.

3 Push the succulents into the sand and compost. Trim the stalks if necessary, so that the base of each succulent sits on the sand.

4 Add a few small shells, pebbles, or gravel around the succulents to finish off the arrangement. Brush the inside of the glass with a paintbrush if necessary, to remove any bits of compost or sand.

# Orchid Falls

The simple rounded shapes of this design perfectly complement the sinuous curves of the orchid and lily flowers. It reminds me of a waterfall that cascades over a tall cliff. Keep all the flower colors fairly neutral, simply to avoid the arrangement looking too fussy.

## FLORALS

- 3 stems of calla lily, tall, medium and short
- 3 sets of two large leaves
- 1 large spray of orchid
- 2 small sprays of orchid
- Spare leaves

## OTHER MATERIALS

- 6 in. (15 cm) Styrofoam® ball
- Serrated knife
- Sheet moss
- Floral U-pins
- Glue gun
- Floral adhesive clay
- Large shallow glass bowl (such as that used as a fish bowl)

1 Cut the ball foam in half down the center with a sharp serrated knife to make two domes.

2 Cover one of the domes with a layer of moss, securing it in place with U-pins.

3 Cover the base of the dome with spare leaves, gluing them in place with dabs of glue from the glue gun.

4 Place a strip of floral adhesive clay in the bottom of the bowl and press the covered dome firmly down onto it.

continued next page

**TIP**
Good quality faux florals are essential here, as the wire inside the stems will allow you to position the flower heads just where you want them.

**5** Start by placing the three lily stems in the center of the dome, arranging them roughly in an arching spray.

**6** Arrange the lilies to face forward and hold them together by twisting a length of floral stem wire around the base of the stems.

**7** Pin a few of the leaf sprigs into position around the base of the lilies.

**8** Place the longer orchid spray towards the back of the arrangement.

*The sinuous curves of the flowers remind me of a waterfall that cascades over a tall cliff...*

**9** Add a lower orchid at the front of the arrangement, curving it over the edge.

**10** Bending the larger orchid stem will allow it to drape gracefully over the edge of the bowl.

**11** Finally, add the curved orchid to one side of the arrangement.

# Blue Notes

For this wonderfully light and airy display you will need to use quite open flower heads and a selection of sweeping foliage. The glass vase has a wide fluted top, which allows the stems to lean outward gracefully rather than bunching up together.

## FLORALS
- 2 stems of blue agapanthus
- 3 stalks of yellow lisianthus
- 3 stalks of very deep purple lisianthus
- 2 stems of bells of Ireland
- 3 stems of lilac
- 1 purple iris
- 4 stalks of red-green berries cut from a bush
- 1 branch of olive-green foliage

## OTHER MATERIALS
- Sheet moss
- Fluted glass vase

1 Push sheet moss firmly down into the bottom of the vase to support the base of the stems. Leave the moss looser at the top so the stems will go into it easily. You can add more moss later if necessary.

2 Place the bells of Ireland stems in the center but slightly toward the back, to establish the overall height of the arrangement.

3 Cut the agapanthus stems so the flowers sit above one another just above the edge of the vase and place them on one side of the bells of Ireland.

4 Add the lilac stem to the opposite side of the vase to balance the agapanthus, and to create color mass here.

**TIP**

If the stems of your flowers are too short for your vase, build up the bottom with some layers of moss to lift the design up a little and allow it to fall naturally.

**5** Place the large iris into the arrangement behind the lilac, to give a little background color at this point in the design.

**6** The yellow and the dark purple lisianthus go in next, spaced out around the design, to add accent colors.

**7** Arrange the berry stems to add some texture and to extend the design out further at the sides.

**8** Finally add foliage around the display to create a background, fill in any gaps, and add texture.

*This wonderfully light and airy display is created with open flower heads and a selection of sweeping foliage...*

# Picture Perfect

Vertical planting is all the rage at the moment and this mini version
is fun to create and will make a great decorative feature. Choose small
succulents and a use a deep-sided frame, adding dried moss to finish the look.

## FLORALS
- Selection of mini faux
  succulents such as
  echeveria, pachyveria,
  sedum hispanicum,
  haworthia, kalanchoe,
  sempervivum, and
  aeonium

## OTHER MATERIALS
- Wooden box, or
  deep-sided frame
  with glass removed
- Paintbrush and
  water-based paint
- Block of Styrofoam®
- Serrated knife
- Glue gun
- Sheet moss
- Scissors or wire
  cutters

**1** Paint the frame, leaving the inside unpainted.
Apply a second coat of paint if necessary, and
leave to dry completely.

**2** Cut pieces of foam to sit snugly inside the frame,
making sure that it will sit below the top edge.

**3** Apply dabs of hot glue to the inside of the frame
and stick the foam in place securely, so that it will
not move.

**4** Cut a piece of moss and glue it on onto the foam
to cover the surface completely, tucking the edges
inside the frame neatly.

**5** Start to put succulents into the frame, starting with the larger ones, gluing them as you go. Try to use different colors and shapes next to each other to add interest to the arrangement.

**6** Continue to push the succulents into the foam and moss, filling any gaps with smaller plants until most of the moss is covered.

# Flower Column

Finding a very tall, thin vase inspired this dramatic column of flowers, which would be an ideal feature display in any room. Remember to try and keep the flowers in a vertical line as much as possible as you place them in the design.

## FLORALS

- 1 green delphinium or hollyhock stem
- 7 open white lily flowers
- 6 white lily buds
- A few stems of green chrysanthemum
- 2 large pink peony
- 2 large olive peony
- 2 sprays of white buddleia

## OTHER MATERIALS

- Small block of Styrofoam®
- Tall china vase

**1** Cut a small piece of foam and push it into the mouth of the vase. Push the end of the delphinium into the foam. Arrange six of the open white lilies around the delphinium in the vase.

**2** Bend over the end of each of the lily bud stems and hook them over the edge of the vase so that the buds hang downward.

**3** Repeat with the last of the open lily stems, trying to keep the arrangement as linear as possible.

**4** Add a few small green chrysanthemums around for additional texture.

**5** Add alternate large pink and olive peonies around the lip of the vase.

**6** Introduce the white buddleia to fill in any gaps and balance the line of the design.

CHAPTER 3

# Gift Ideas

Don't forget about the containers you may already
have—and you don't necessarily have to use a "vase" in
order to create a great arrangement. Think outside the box!
What do you have, maybe a pitcher, an old wooden
box, a teapot? Be creative. In this chapter we focus
on using a wide variety of alternative bases—and
in one of the projects you will actually create
the container too!

# Daisy Display

Even though this design only uses one flower, by grouping it together in a set of three you can see how it becomes a striking display with impact. Here I have used a colorful votive candleholder as the "vase," since each individual arrangement is tiny and so needs a small container for balance. The colors in the glass also went together so well with the flowers.

**FLORALS**
- 3 gerbera daisy flowers

**OTHER MATERIALS**
- Clear glass marbles
- Small multicolored glass pieces (or use colored glass beads for jewelry)
- 3 small glass votive candleholders

**1** Cut the stem of the flower down quite short so the head of the flower will sit a short distance above the container.

**2** Choose the smallest glass marbles for this project, as the container is very small.

**3** Shape the stem into a gentle curve with your fingers so it will face outward. Place the end of the stem down in the container.

**4** Fill around the stem with clear glass marbles to hold it securely in place. Add a few multicolored glass pieces on top of the clear glass marbles.

# Tulip Window Box

Silk flowers can be used outside as well, as long as they are placed in a sheltered position where they will not be in harsh sun or get wet in rain. This elegant trough with its marching line of tulips would make an ideal windowsill display.

## FLORALS
- 5 yellow-orange tulips
- 12 sprays of forsythia
- 1 ivy bush divided down into sprays

## OTHER MATERIALS
- Styrofoam® block
- Serrated knife
- Sheet moss
- Floral U-pins
- Decorative metal trough

### TIP
If your faux florals have wired petals, you can choose just how open you want the flowers to be. Bend the wire gently with your fingers and smooth the petals into an attractive shape.

1 Cut the foam to fit the trough and cover it in moss as described on page 28.

2 Place the tulips to establish the shape of the design (two in front, three in back).

3 Add the sprigs of forsythia along the edges to fill in below the tulip flowers, spacing them roughly equally.

4 Arrange the sprigs of ivy around the edge of the container, draping it artfully down so it falls over the sides of the trough.

# Harvest Flowers

This cheerful arrangement is made up of bright sunflowers and poppies, with berries and fall foliage for a real feeling of the fall harvest. The stainless steel metal pail seemed an ideal container, but I painted it white to soften its metallic color.

## FLORALS
- 4 sunflowers
- I sunflower bud
- 3 orange-red poppies
- I yellow poppy
- 2 yellow cosmos
- 2 orange zinnias
- Trailing spray of leaves
- 3 sprays of bittersweet berries
- 4 sprays of dark berries
- 2 sprays of fall foliage

## OTHER MATERIALS
- 6 in. (15 cm) Styrofoam® ball
- Sheet moss
- Floral U-pins
- Glue gun
- Metal vase or bucket

**1** Prepare the base by painting the bucket if desired. Place a Styrofoam® ball in the top and cover with moss as described on page 28. Add a trailing stem of leaves, tucking the ends up into the moss.

**2** Place the tall orange-red poppies in the center of the arrangement to establish the height, then set the sunflowers around in a circle.

**3** Add more poppies, zinnias, and cosmos, using them to fill in any gaps between the sunflowers and the poppies.

**4** Place the berries in the arrangement symmetrically to add texture. Finish by placing some fall foliage around the base of the design.

# Pitcher of Roses

To create this charming and informal arrangement of roses, you will need at least three different shades of flowers in any color that you prefer. The roses add mass to the design while the arching white stems add shape, movement, and further interest to the display.

## FLORALS

- 2 yellow open roses
- 3 yellow rosebuds
- 6 pink variegated open roses
- 1 variegated rosebud
- 2 dark pink open roses
- 1 dark pink rosebud
- 3 white rosebuds
- 5 arching white flower stems
- 6 white filler stems

## OTHER MATERIALS

- Large clear glass chunks
- Pack of clear acrylic water
- 1 glass pitcher

### TIP

If you do not want to permanently set the flowers in a vase that you consider special, simply omit the acrylic water and add more marbles to stabilize the rose stems.

1 Mix the acrylic water following the manufacturer's instructions. Half-fill the base of a pitcher with marbles and acrylic water.

2 Place strips of tape over the top of the pitcher in a criss-cross pattern.

3 Start building the arrangement by threading the flowers through the gaps in the tape, to make a pleasing rounded shape.

4 Fill in any gaps around the edge with filler stems and arching white stems to add movement and style to the design.

# Teatime Flowers

If you are into recycling, this is the ideal project for you! The container is a teapot that is missing its lid and the flowers are individual blooms left over from other arrangements. Add a few blooms to the side of the pot to break up the bottom edge of the design.

1 Place the piece of foam point down into the teapot so it just protrudes—if it is too long, cut off the tip so you can push the cone further into the teapot, rather than trying to slice off the top.

2 Trim the hydrangea flowers heads back a little, otherwise the arrangement may be too full for the teapot.

3 Glue the small blue hydrangea flower heads onto the sides of the teapot to break up the straight line of the top of the pot.

4 Arrange the first peony bloom to establish the focal point of the arrangement.

**5** Add the second peony on the other side, then the cream hydrangeas.

**6** Finish off with the peony buds, using them to fill in any gaps in the design.

# Hyacinth Basket

If you don't have the right container for your display, it is often quite easy to create your own. For this display of hyacinths, the "basket" is simply two large blocks of foam glued together, covered with a layer of Spanish moss and decorated with dried twigs.

## FLORALS
- 9 hyacinth blooms
- 4 or 5 sprigs of English ivy
- 10 stems of grass
- 6 sprigs of daisy flowers

## OTHER MATERIALS
- Spanish moss
- Reindeer moss
- Large selection of dried twigs
- Two large rectangular blocks of Styrofoam®
- Craft glue
- Floral U-pins
- Glue gun
- Wire cutters

1 Spread craft glue over the side of one block of foam. Stick the two blocks together to make one large, rectangular block.

2 Pile a layer of Spanish moss over one side of the foam block and secure it in place with the U-pins.

### TIP
If you don't have suitable twigs for this project you can dismantle a wreath and snip it down into suitable lengths.

3 Cut the twigs roughly to the height of the block with the wire cutters.

4 Carefully put a line of hot glue down one side of a twig.

continued next page

**TIP**
You could also use
popsicle sticks or craft
sticks instead of the twigs
for the sides of your
basket, to give a less
rustic look.

**5** Press the twig down onto the moss, lining up the ends with the bottom edge of the foam as you work. Cover all four sides of the foam block in this way.

**6** Add a layer of reindeer moss across the top of the block, then use the wire cutters to snip the top ends of the twigs off in line with the top of the block.

**7** Pin the sprigs of ivy at intervals around the edge of the basket.

**8** Since their stems are quite thick, make a guide hole in the foam for each hyacinth with a pencil.

*Sprigs of grass added between the hyacinth
blooms will open out the design and make it
lighter and more airy...*

**9** Add the hyacinths, spacing them roughly equally down the length of the basket with three in the front, three in the middle, and three in the back.

**10** Place some sprigs of grass in between the hyacinth blooms to make the design lighter and more airy.

**11** Finally, add the daisy sprigs at the base of the display.

# Peony and Rose Centerpiece

Stately white peonies and roses are arranged to create a classic ball of blooms in a tall pilsner glass. It is always worth looking at other types of glassware you may have to hand—rather than just your standard vases—when you are initially planning your design.

## FLORALS
- 4 stems of white peony
- 7 full-bloom white or cream roses
- 2 white or cream rosebuds

## OTHER MATERIALS
- Pack of clear acrylic water
- Pilsner glass or tall narrow vase

### TIP
If you are making a centerpiece for a dining table, don't choose a high design like this. Make something low so people can see each other across the table.

1 Prepare the vase by mixing the acrylic water and adding it to the vase as described on page 29. Remove any leaves that are too low down.

2 Start by placing one open rose in the center of the vase, to establish the highest point in your design.

3 Add a second rose to the middle, next to the first one, then place four open roses equally spaced around the outside of the vase.

4 Fill in the gaps in the design using the peonies, spacing them equally around the bouquet. Add the remaining roses. Leave in a warm place for the acrylic water to set.

# Poppy Bowl

The splash of color from these red poppies can brighten up the dullest corner of any room. Shallow bowls like this can be used for taller arrangements by fixing foam in the base to hold the blooms securely in place. I particularly like the natural organic feel of this design.

**FLORALS**
- 5 red poppy stems with a mixture of flowers and buds

**OTHER MATERIALS**
- Piece of Styrofoam®
- Floral adhesive clay
- Sandpaper block
- Glue gun (optional)
- Pebbles
- Shallow stoneware bowl

1 Cut the sides of the foam at an angle so it will fit into the container better. Smooth cut edges with sandpaper. Place strips of waterproof floral adhesive clay in the base of the bowl and press the shaped block of foam down firmly onto it. Fill any gaps around the edge with odd bits of foam.

2 Cover the foam entirely with a handful of natural colored pebbles. If you prefer, you can secure the pebbles in place with dabs of glue, but wait until the design is finished first.

3 Place the tallest poppy stem in the foam to establish the height of the design.

4 Add another tall stem at the rear of the arrangement, then place a shorter flower toward the front.

**5** Next, place some additional foliage to fill in the center of the arrangement.

**6** Finally, fill in any large gaps with the remaining flowers, keeping the design quite open and airy.

# Pastel Perfection Bowl

A simple cream stoneware mixing bowl makes an unusual base for this selection of pastel spring flowers. Although the flowers are different colors they are quite similar in tone, so it is the varied shapes and textures that are creating the main interest in this arrangement.

## FLORALS

- 3 stems of blue iris stems
- 3 small forsythia sprays
- 3 yellow daffodils
- 10 sprays of purple bells cut from a bush
- 1 fully open white lilac spray
- 1 lilac bud stem
- 1 purple lilac
- 1 spray yellow chrysanthemum
- 4 sprays of purple buddleia
- 1 spray blue accent flower
- Sprays of ivy cut from a bush
- 3 sprays of lavender
- 2 viburnum heads

## OTHER MATERIALS

- 6 in. (15 cm) Styrofoam® ball
- Serrated knife
- Sheet moss
- Floral U-pins
- Glue gun
- White china mixing bowl

**1** Prepare the base by cutting the Styrofoam® ball in half as described on page 86, and then glue it into the bowl.

**2** Cut the iris stems to small, medium, and long lengths and place them in the center of the display to establish the height of the arrangement.

**3** Start adding white viburnum flowers at the lower edge to fill in below the iris blooms.

**4** Add the spray of open white lilac toward the back of the arrangement.

continued next page

**5** Begin introducing contrast colors with the forsythia sprays, then add the yellow daffodils.

**6** Introduce texture and shape by adding some sprays of lavender.

**TIPS**

Stoneware mixing bowls come in a range of sizes and designs, so look out for interesting ones in department stores and flea markets.

Any bowl would look great for this design—even a glass one, as the Styrofoam® base is fully covered with moss

**7** Next, place the four buddleia stems roughly symmetrically at each side of the arrangement.

**8** The arching sprays of purple bells add a sense of movement and lightness to the design. Cut a few sprigs of ivy and arrange them to fill in any gaps and drape artfully over the edge of the bowl.

*It is the varied shapes
and textures that are creating the
main interest...*

# Summer Flowers Basket

Often I take a basket with me when I pick flowers—it's something I've carried over from my childhood. This basket is a bit of a mixed selection, so it is an ideal project to do with all the flowers left over from other projects. The strong shape of the basket and the ivy are the elements that hold the design together.

## FLORALS
- 3 stems of white peony
- 2 stem of white lilac
- 3 sprays of forsythia
- 3 stems of yellow daffodil
- 1 spray of yellow chrysanthemum
- 2 long stems of green-white geranium with leaves
- 1 spray of small pink lilies
- 1 pink tulip
- 3 sprays of pinks
- 2 stems of pink ranunculus
- 5 arching sprays of pink-purple bells
- 1 long spray of green ivy cut from a bush
- Short sprigs of variegated and plain ivy cut from a bush
- 1 long spray of green vine cut from a bush

## OTHER MATERIALS
- Large sheet of Styrofoam®
- Pencil
- Serrated knife
- Sheet moss
- Floral U-pins
- Floral stem wire
- Glue gun
- Wicker basket with handle

1 Set the basket on the sheet of foam and draw around the base with a pencil to get the correct size and shape of foam to cut out. Cut out the foam shape with a serrated knife.

2 Place the foam in the bottom of the basket and cover with moss as described on page 28. Twine a length of ivy down the handle, fixing with wire in inconspicuous places.

3 Adjust the leaves of the ivy as you are winding the vine down the handle so that they look natural and attractive. Keep them in place with a dab of glue.

4 Add some sprigs of variegated and plain ivy around the sides of the basket so they drape artfully down over the edge.

continued next page

TIPS

If your basket is a bit misshapen you can soak it in water for 12 hours until the wicker softens, then reshape and allow it to dry. Don't try this with lacquered or varnished wicker though—and remove any added decorations before you soak.

When you pick flowers from the garden you don't always have the choice of taking an even number in one type. In this project it is fine to use one type of flower on one side of an arrangement and on the other side to use a different variety of flower as long as is a similar size and color.

For an additional country feel, you may wish to add a decorative bow to the handle of the basket.

**5** Place the peonies at each side and the white lilac in the center to set the height and width of the arrangement.

**6** Add the forsythia around the center lilac to add some color and texture, and start building mass.

**7** Place a few more yellow daffodils and tiny chrysanthemums to add yellow accents.

**8** Add the pink lilies, tulip, and ranunculus around the sides to fill in any gaps.

*Often I take a basket with me when I pick flowers—it's something I've carried over from my childhood...*

9 Next, the long stems of white geraniums are positioned at the top of the arrangement on each side of the basket.

10 Add a couple of sprays of pinks to the arrangement at each end, then the sprays of bells on either side to add movement.

11 Finally, tuck the end of a spray of ivy into the basket at one side, curve it around the front of the basket and tuck the end into the edge of the arrangement on the other side.

# Index

# Acknowledgments

I would like to dedicate this book to my husband, Dana, my kids, and my family. Thank you for allowing me to spend countless hours in the studio during the making of this book. I really do have the most wonderfully supportive family.

A special thanks goes to the staff of Martin Floral for assisting me in the selection of these beautiful flowers.

# Suppliers

## US

Afloral.com
www.afloral.com

Artificial Plants, Trees & Flowers
www.artificialplantsandtrees.com

Fiori Belli
www.fioribelli.com

Floral Supplies & more
www.floralsuppliesandmore.com

Nearly Natural
www.nearlynatural.com

Petals
www.petals.com

Quality Silk Plants
www.qualitysilkplants.com

Quality Silks
www.qualitysilks.com

USI Floral Inc.
www.usifloral.com

## Canada

House of Silk
www.houseofsilk.ca

Portage Flowers
www.portageflowers.ca

## UK

Abigail Ahern
www.abigailahern.com

Amazon
www.amazon.co.uk

Artificial Plants
www.artificialplants.co.uk

Bloom
www.bloom.uk.com

Decoflora
www.silkflowersdecoflora.co.uk

Fake Landscapes
www.fake.com

GT Decorations
www.gtdecorations.com

John Lewis
www.johnlewis.com

Just Artificial
www.justartificial.co.uk

Props 4 Shows,
www.props4shows.co.uk

Peony
www.peony.co.uk

Sara Richards Flowers
www.sara-richards.co.uk

Withycombe Fair
www.withycombefair.co.uk

Wyld Home,
www.wyldhome.com

## Australia

Austwan
www.austwan.com

Flowerama
www.flowerama.net.au

Silk Flowers
www.silkflowers.com.au